LOVE

in the wintertime

DON GUTTERIDGE

ISBN 0 88750 810 3 (hardcover)
ISBN 0 88750 811 1 (softcover)

Typesetting and design by Michael Macklem

Printed in Canada

PUBLISHED IN CANADA BY OBERON PRESS

Part 1: Love and Other Griefs

SOLILOQUY, FOR LOVERS

(For my mother and father, in memoriam)

I

Come with me, our paired blades
snare cadence, the ice
horizonless: we will dare passage

    I am scared: of the free-fall ice
    lends, of freedom and bondage

Once I skated alone to the village-edge
beyond the eave of the last shanty
over marsh-ice the moon's
elemental glow reduced to diamond
these skates shredded in frenzy,
I tell you there was no pivot-point
but the carbon-dark of my breathing

    I saw you first, gladiatorial, teething
    on cheers, you couldn't guess my need
    for grace in the nub of violence, blood
    on your brow stirs in me
    something retrieved from summer

The cheers surround me, urge surrender,
like a village they would take possession
with applause—I open flesh
with a stick, its blood is green:
I will not show cause

7

They see the act, male and outlaw,
I recognize the deed, the girl
shyness in the shape of your skating,
lust propelling every dance
we disguise it from, after all
I wound the ground I walk on

I saw you first, an eye stalking me,
estranged; your voice orphan,
your plaudit predatory, yet something
akin to winter in it, the victor
fox made victim by the cold

Let ours be a summer-love, propelled
by the winters that close it in

Let ours be a winter-love, mocked
by the summers that shut it out

2

I never dreamt a February courting,
the moon passionate in black,
snow lush against sill and eave,
trees amnesiac over burrows
our bodies forge with their warmth:
love, like the village driven
inward to the pivot-point,
is lit with its own element

I am stunned by gentleness,
yours and my own, the ice
on the shanty walls en*trances*—
the lake mocks us with its miles,
I want to skate its distance
to death, take you utterly
into aloneness, make us both
orphans in a new world

    I have that part of you curled
    inside me, the eaves are breathing

I am afraid of your ease,
of freedom and bondage

    I love you
    I will not hold it hostage

I love you
I give you this village

    Let us believe the future

Let us share passage

    Let the dance be mutual

BETWEEN THE WARS

One day in the winter of '37
my father's eye caught the
furtive star in my mother's:
for a moment the snow stayed cozy,
lust offered her surrogate warmth
to lovers foolish enough
to let their dreams fraternize,
to bear the wonder of it all
nine months later when I
surprised the wastage
                     of the world.

But, alas, they loved me too much
to tell me there was no future.

PATSY: THE SILENCE

(For Patsy Cline, in memory)

For you a song was not a thing
to be bruised musical,
gourmandized in the gritty
serenade you served
your worshippers nightly.

For you a song was not the soul's
hungering to be unorphaned
in winged epiphanies
or the appetite for applause.

For you a song was something
shadowed and intricately under:
a lyric air in the brassy sax,
for example, or something
serenely sexed and renegade
in the belly of the brain
and avid for any exit.

You lived your life that way,
each song, crooned and sirened
in the blue laser of fame,
was only halfway yours, a reaching
beyond for what's been lost
already before belonging.

Until the day you took the sky
for breath / surrogate lung,
your lover's grip upon the Cessna's
throttle, you aimed a tender wing
against the sheerest perpendicular,
O you hammered brass/tongued flesh/
the tuning-bone in your throat
upon the effortless air, you
drank the carnivore cry
                    of your own death.

While we: merely alive, condemned to endure
(against the taciturnities of time)
the silence of all the songs you'll never sing.

GOOD MEASURE

I am merman

with my one
eyed fin
is all
    swim

in the well
come water

    And what purpose
    O smooth-skinned
    porpoise who are
    all heart
    beating up
           channel?

I seek the
sea-home
Odysseus al-
most missed

    Penelope is
    no prize, seaman,
    even for your
    size

She's the
womb of man—
woman—the sea-
sons reproduce

Circe, you mean
who sang for her supper
(cutlets, I think)
on her poisoned littoral

What are *you* serving,
                        sailor?

I offer up
my eye
like Oedipus

Like Lucifer
catching Eve
in the raw

. . . in the dappled after-
math I deny
all pleasure

So do I,
but for good measure
I'm keeping
            the apple

14

GUINEVERE'S CONUNDRUM

Make your mind up
for Chrissake,
will it be
ageing Arthur
and his trained seal
or randy Lance
the untutored pup?

Arthur, always

Braced in his kingsgrip
I am offered Englands,
battles on the sea-
tower of Tintagel
and I am the
woman by the well:
draw him down
he takes me up,
together we come
to the high kingdom

Hurry up, will you?
I can't switch metre
in mid-rhythm!

Lancelot, always

It is you who are
Merlin's brat,
you with the secrets
of the nether cave,
I sucked them out of you
and sent you forth
to your first wars
                    a stallion

You brought me back
the face of a future king

and squandered it

So,
I let you quest
without compunction
in the queen's flesh,
bade you plunder
without sacrilege
the treasured vessels
of the fiefdom

I played the princess, earth
mother, dark lady to your
make-believe gallantry

In the king's chamber
I spread my thighs
to make the only cup
you could ever enter

When you were gone
I dreamt of sea-
urchins, underwater grottoes
and Merlin
wielding his wand

See, I can balance you
like a ball on my
pope's nose!
            Don't fall

Arthur, always

For him I become
stirrup, scabbard,
wine-pouch, pillow
on the bronze throne
for his ageing head

At the climax
of our rare love
he feels again
the warrior's death-clench
the blood that strokes a sword,
his fierce protagonist's heart

Afterwards
I bathe my lord's eyes
with worshipping:
they're like the stars
straightened by Stonehenge
and
on my breasts: his hands
perpetually dreaming
                    a grail

I love you:
with God's love
for Christ's sake

ABELARD'S PLEA

Headache again?

   No, the nunnery

   I have grown to love
   the chaste walls
   I look upon
   with impunity,
   the snowdrops un-
   visited by bees,
   the tufted greenery
   of my June garden,
   the fresh light
   along these sills
   to see the world by

It was so good
last time, you do
remember, don't you?

Too long between letters—
the summers you confected
with words, tropes, the
rhythms imprisoned
in your cleft flesh
I caught with my
virgin's blood, turned
inward to spring
outward to hope

or the winters you etched
with trochee, iambic,
metaphors of despair
that made me somehow
whisper
  spero
  sperandum est

What do you think
I am, a eunuch?

No, never that

For years I husbanded
the joy of our first union,
nursed it with a child's
wild hunger till it
grew eloquent
in its own light

Something I said, then?

Yes, and not said

I need symbols, gestures,
verbs in the future tense,
nouns to sharpen the
distance between us,
unleash the seasons
to pain and poetry

I love you
I *love* you

Not enough

I'm sitting upright
in the cloistered light

Upon the intact
wall of my memory
I scratch with this
crooked crayon
the first
       blood-budding
              obscenity

LOVE: IN WINTERTIME

(For George Amabile)

I

Look, love,
my eskimo bone-
sword straightens the
undecodable curves
this snow confounds
our earth with!

I build you a cave:
curves of our own
as tender as a belly
before love, its props
the sturdy consonants I
carve your name with—

let it be
nave and chapel
chamber and hearth
till that other season
                    come.

For now, your presence
renders it "home"

But—
I am the igloo
(shadow-warmth
the ugly feather-
ridden hen)

For a while I'll
play the little whore
you lose your warrior's
heart to,

but—
it's *my* skin
the winter wind
                    leathers

For you I'll be
the harpoon flung
at Nanook's
moon-dark heart,
the chiselled fist
bloody in the wolves'
arctic hunger

For you
I would bay
at the Pleiades

> I too can please
> I'll improvise
> the hidden sun
> who plants improper
> blisses on each of your
> icicle kisses

> Don't run, there's fun
> in fiery improprieties!

2

Our mounded house
I shield against the sky's
absolute zero

like Samson heartened
by his agonies
like Atlas guarding
the green alphabet
at the world's deadening
                    edge

   A snowbank is no hedge:
   Eve chose the apple
   round as a rump
   redder than a blush
   plucked Eden from her eye
   for such fecundity—

   if there is knowledge
   in unnameable tundra
   in the frigid rose,
   I too will choose:
   let its bitten crystal's
   flowering blood
   extinguish my cry

3

You beg for the Petrarchan
language of lovers,
but on the annihilating
snowscape of our bower
the mutual sonnet dies,
even the graceful letters
of your name come unfettered,
the consonants of love resurrect
their immaculate anonymity,
the vowels marooned in a
blizzard of stars:

the world's without conjunction—
I howl love
with my barbar's tongue!

In a universe
without predicate
you hammer out
aboriginal grammars
on the tablet of my tongue—

From the clench of desire
you manufacture "lust"
from the forceps of my lips
you confect "lick" and "suck,"
the foam of my thighs
tosses them high
onto Aphrodite's wave,
and the woman-words
I reach for (with my eyes,
with the bones I long to
curl about you like tendrils,
with the flesh I chill
into hope's chalice)
slither
          to the lunar
side of silence

Abandoned on these barrens
bereft of all gods
we will erect prisms

to the north of December,
dream cathedrals
with tree-tall spires
in the secular wind,
a tallow-lit altar
we spread our ease upon
like shaman's robes
unblessed by priests

Into the solstice-silence
I drop the syllable-seed
your body hoards
against the unspeakable

Together we wait
for some future
to remember
            its voice

    I have no choice:

    unbidden, the child
    sleeps in the wordless
    dream of borrowed flesh,

    when it wakes
    somewhere south of Eden
    I will not rejoice

    though its cry
    be as tender
    as the touch
            of tomorrow

Part 2: Family Resemblance: An Album

AFTERIMAGE

(For Anne)

No lover's eye
could cope with the
girl in the Volkswagen's
sigh against the curb:

a wince of
lemon dress,
red hair
piled high,
flesh pebbled with
mother-of-pearl and a
smile hinting
hope in the
   May sky

(but I try)

"Hi," you say,
"It's time we flew!"

And we do

31

COURAGE

(For John)

Ten months you hover
under the ice, and
for a second I
wonder what courage
it takes to brave
the air, to risk
oblivion for the
urge-to-be.

Later, under glass
the head is a lop-
sided bludgeon
(mother-blood undried)
but the right eye
gleams with the
hope it has won

I'm me,
it states

And skates.

FLEDGLING

(For Kate)

Featherless and
rubbed red
by the raw womb—
nevertheless
in your fledgling eye
terse and blue:
the will to fly.

A daughter,
said the nurse
unwittingly, who
did not see the
swoop of your glance
acknowledge the air,
then me

Hello, it said
I'm new

And flew.

SKETCHING ANNE

(Christmas morning, 1982)

If I were to draw you
in lines more loving than words,
they would be Varley's
quickened curves
sketching the essence of
girl in the raw
morning's moment
after love.

But then I
am no Varley, and you
no longer a girl
to be the essence
                          of

Take heart,
draw me closer:
it's time we measured
these ageing pleasures
without rhyme.

TO A DAUGHTER, WRITING
HER FIRST POEM

Twice nine months
we waited for the
word to stir, ravel,
utter itself to
                    air:
the first gospel
from that little body's
acrobatic syllabics
we worshipped
                    with listening.

For a time, though,
you were content
with the coupling chime
of somersault and the
whees of joy your breath
gave back in rhyme,
we held our own
in awe, in hope
as you flipped dactyls,
spun gymnastic
letters of love
to the everywhere
                    around

you mailed your circular
sonnets to yourself
and we loved you
loving them.

At twelve, you stilled:
the will-to-meaning
shamed to silence,
the flesh clenched
on the unutterable
comprehending no
lyric of girlhood
could assuage.

Then: pen on the
precipice of the page—
scapular, scourging,
blood-propelled,
you grip the leveraging
trapeze of a poem
and aim your self
beyond *to be, now*

                    or *ever*

SOUTHAMPTON SUMMER

(For Anne and for Jack Chambers,
in memory)

With separate breath
again we watch the
Southampton sun
draw first blood
across the raw sketch
where water and sky
discompose.

And no memory
however shared or sweet
(of stretched sands
brushed by dew-light,
of children's cries
wombed in blue
forever noon,
of gooseflesh dunes
under the unpigmented moon,
of evenings bequeathed to
lovers/stars/the etch
of bonfires embering) —
no such memory,
unbidden or discreetly
recomposed, can lay
the ghosts we've raised
merely by wanting to be,
and be remembering.

Take my hand:
look due west
where the heart dips inward,
let us retrieve for ourselves
that lost, once child-
horizoned Huron summer
Jack Chambers drew
for us
    and the world.

38

VOYAGEURS: MUSKOKA, JUNE 1981

(For Gerry Parker and Allan Gedalof)

For three slaphappy days
we dip our professorial paddles
into storied waters, play
Champlain and Groseilliers
to our own applause,
assault Muskokan portages
miming the heathen voyageurs
who scandalized our schoolbook,
and in the umber of evening
over birchflame and brandy
we immemorialize the Bard's best,
decant a bawdy song or two,
and marvel at the chance marriage
of time and the particular flesh.

Until the night we encamp
on Black Lake's rock-promontory
older than Adam or God's
dream of artful Eve:
we lie upright along the dark
listening rigid
        to the pterodactyl laughter
        of loons' decoupling dance
        while the bachelor stars above
        hallucinate paternity
        and the moon like a
        wall-eyed troubador
        unweaves
        Earth's epic silence.

HYMN TO THE BLUE-EYED UNBORN

(For my grandson Tom, born on May Day, 1985)

Even then
nine-months' deep in the
memory of the womb you
clung to some nub of hope
as inward you grew unleafing
infant filigree against
the featureless ocean of
ambience and seasonable
blue-dream, you spun
yourself perfect, unique
in that unambitious ether
till an urge more ancient than love
(or merely some homely music
you might have heard beckon
from the sea beyond the sea)
propelled you leewardly down—
and blood-ruddered, butterfly-
boned, braving anyway
you uncocooned yourself
and entered Adam's crippled air.

Even now
out of the incubator's stunted breath
amidst a galaxy of tubes and clicking digits—
only your argonaut's eye is free to have its say:

    you give us, once and quick,
    the womb's blue glance

What else can we do
but whisper it back
and be blessed
           in the utterance.

MADONNA AND CHILD: CHRISTMAS 1986

(For Anne and Tom)

Into the grandmothering
cradle of your elder's arms
you take our doubting Thomas
and the room composes around you:

the wintering sun, stilled,
enrobes your beauty
in prism and fold,
your hair as virgin
as the silled snow
made bolden by

a holly's blood-berry,
the wandering jew
against the pastured glass,
a thorn-rose, clipped
in a blue vase

you encompass them all—
like the child's cry from the loft
soothed in the deft
revival of a smile.

The room resumes its breathing now, as it should,
Baby-Tom, past all doubting now, sleeps—
and dreams, once again, that the world is good.

TOM'S SONG

(For my grandson, at 18 months)

Out of the ribbed cradle you croon
the alphabet of your becoming,
each syllable you bend celibate
and cadenced out of your boy's
being once and now
(singsong, rhyme-wild, zany
as the moon's cow)
then unrehearse yourself again
just for the joy of/a newness of
the morning's blue breath
that wafts it wingless
against my ageing ear

I let it soar orphaned
into the resident dream:

    full of Afghans
    scorched in their crib
    and Ethiopian bloat
    and lullabies detongued
    among the world's rubble

I wake wide with my poet's eye
I crave rage
I beg the absent gods
to let me go loon-mad,
like Tom's song I long just once
to be what I un-am
before the all-anger blooms unassuaged
in the bent fury of the word.

TO ALL SCOTTISH TERRIERS
NAMED MARGARET

(And to the memory of one in particular,
Margaret Isabelle Cooper, 1975-1987)

You bore your Christian name
with a sufferance befitting
the aboriginal Scots committee
who surmised that you and your kind
were a plot against petdom
and the lapdog English

You named only yourself,
ignored slight of
outsize snout or
slur of midget
wrestler's feet,
and caring nothing for the
impedimenta of your
unmatched pedigree parts
you gave full cry
to the antic terrier-heart:

    flinging that highland howl
    among the English squirrels
    treed in their terror
    above the glens of Gibbon's Park
    (a country mile from Culloden)
    and
    outbreasting whippets and winded Danes
    (surprised by the sheer
    glee of speed)
    you leave them rollicking
    in a dazed wake

(yet never fail to pause,
pirouette on the axis
of your whisker-tail
and suffer our patronizing
outsize applause)

We love you
for the stand-up comic
days you gave us
to recall you by
in ceremonial laughter.

But mostly we love you
because you stood for all
those midget hopefuls among us
who—encumbered though they be
with bone-and-brawn
they had no hand in making—
nonetheless let fly
the frantic fancy
to while
            and prevail.

And for that other rarer prize
unique to the Margaret breed:
      the clumsy dignity of the country clown
      too wise for the smile beneath the frown.

EVE: THE MYSTERIES

(For Anne, Christmas, 1988)

I

The garden must have been
Galapagos rampant with
tanagers and the skirr
of malignant humming
birds and herring gulls
with pterodactyl urges
and tortoises slouching sunward
on the oyster-strewn beach
where neutered iguanas
ponder etymology
and pythons swoon
in the eucalyptus
whose boreal gloom is
lit with iridescence of
orchid, moon-coral,
the lustrous sea-conch—
this island without synonym:
Eve's uninnocent demesne.

(No upstart Jehovah here
with hegemonic smile to
clutter creation with language—
and nary an apple tree for miles!)

Ungrammared she stands
beauteous amid beauty
in absolute unreflexion

(nor anyone to ripple
with gazing that image
or catechize the dream
she dreams herself dreaming in)

2

Adam, of course, was never cohabitant
(inserted later by propheteers
anxious to keep our myths domestic).
The truth is this:
smitten with a life sentence
he spent his youth
unbaptized and pole-
vaulting on a spare rib
over back-garden walls
from Aden to Amherstburg,
desperate for one glimpse
of iridescence
or apple unbitten.

3

Like most of his sons, though,
I am content
to hold you close
(full-ribbed, beloved)
and let the tangents
of that ancient dream
touch as they will—
all their Mysteries
            blissfully unresolved.

FIRSTBORN

(For William John)

I

Even the forceps' bite
couldn't bid you wave
goodbye to that
dolphin-wise world
you curled inside and
unimperilled sang
(with a blood-lung)
soliloquies to the
whale-wide sea
of your beginning.

The firstborn
bears the indelible
weight of naming
as, our own hope ageing,
we christen you scion
son, proud paladin
of our doubled lineage.

And you still
good in your growing
assumed the likeness
we drew of you
as our lusts jelled

and after a while
even the names of the
ancient monarchs
we crowned you with
began to shape
their sounds around
the smile you used
to disarm the air—
the grin
of your shy disguise.

So that even we—
who loved you into being
and boyhood and the
man you've made for us—
might fail to hear
(as we ought) the ache
of dolphins
　　　　　singing
　　　　　　　　anthems
of aloneness in the Undersea.

52

SAY UNCLE

*(For my uncle, Bob Gutteridge, on
the occasion of his 65th birthday)*

I

In a wartime village
starved of fathers and
teeming with kids' need
for gun-hipped heroes
to harvest their boy-bravery,
you were the elder
surrogate brother,
the cowboy-commando
who never said uncle.

O how we cheered
your home-run waltz
your swagger on rink-
quickened blades,
your quarterback's stutterstep
outwitting our clumsy
capture in every scene
that ended in your imp's grin,
the conspirator's wink
we took as adulterous blessing
as the rapture of inclusion
in the game about-to-be-played
somewhere just beyond the
fission of sky and
blood-linked sun.

And so we mimicked
and marched and mimed
your hungering and fed
our enthusiasm for oblivion
and happy endings—
till the day you rode
wilfully into the sunset
(where baby-faced snipers
grieve in the cinematic dark)

2

Wars cease, heroes come back
to famished applause,
I grew tall, oddly
ordinary, but you
(imp's laugh scotched,
abaft) had the courtesy
to remain avuncular,
as big as the dream-uncle
in my grandson's blue eye.

Somehow
you kept the "kid-in-you"
intact, beyond age or
the sniper's felicity,
and even now (65 and
grateful for the years
that numb and cauterize)
you pass it generously
down the generations
of nephews and childhood lore:
it is the cause,
the hope you fought for.

3

May you prosper
here among those you love
and there
amid the vast village
of stars and fostering suns.

PRENUPTIALS

(For Erin Pettit, daughter-in-law-to-be)

I

The goddess who named you first
must have been dreaming of
emerald glens and fairy-rings
round the maypole dance
where the self-effacing
reticence of elves-eyes
shy as shamrock, sings
amidst the oceans-old
                    Gaelic grace.

2

Maybe so.

For even as we translate them
with the story of our lives
the names we bear at our birth
are as true as the bones
we grow with or the vows
we swear from time to time
as testament to love's
                    fragility.

And after all,
your presence in the
hubbub of a room
is the kind of music
nobody notes till
the din palls and
we wake to the gloam
of a troubled morning:
our blood humming
melodic
          with gentle remembrance.

And sure as Heaven
the diffident beauty
of your just-being
would have stirred
the Celtic bards
to celebrate love
with lute-sweet
                    lustiness.

3

Maybe so.

Still, we must admit
those names you've kept
for yourself only
(as we all do)
hoarded warm in the
chrysalid of expectation:
    precious and terrible
    beyond the telling.

O do not falter now:
let each of your names
become what they will—
and merge with the
words of our welcoming
(O daughter-to-be),
a music for our mutual
                    future.

Part 3: The Loretta Lynn Suite

SONG

(For Sharon and Ian Underhill)

I

From its nest in the
last uninfested
elm, the upside-down orchard
oriole bends her body into
song the
        incipient dusk
momentarily hesitates
then rides upon

Everywhere the trees succumb
to the featureless gloom—

only you with a hum of
waferous bones, skull
ringing like a Sunday
belfry, throat taut
as a lover's tuning-fork,
without design or artifice
against the malignant night
fling
        your lyric of light

2

The image I hold of you
is not Nashville—

I see you at thirteen already dreaming
music out of your father's tarred lungs
music out of the misery of your mother's eyes
music out of ruptured hills the sun
still tints green with memory
music out of the territorial dialect—

the vowels stretched and rounded
to meet the dream your forebears
brought to these speechless valleys,
the consonants hoarded/honed/brandished
against Yankees, revenuers, carpetbaggers,
McCoys, company men and all the do-gooding
social reformers hell-bent to flatten every
accent between Goose Bay and Butcher Holler

and making
music out of your own splintered virginity
music out of a child's body pummelled by love
out of a nine-month belly bevelled by love
out of little-girl grace transformed by love
into song

3

The image I make of you
is this:

You are Keats' nightingale
swallowed by song
keeping history and
innocence as pure as
Ruth's pristine cry,
though the *words* be
our own currency

Words we share
the blame for,
words your voice
reminds us of:
carried intact as
oriole's aboriginal
stammer on the
                    evening air

words that tear
your girl's face
into age, care
little for the love
we bring to heal
you with, spare
no flesh in their
foraging for the future.

But even now
you smile from memory,
the song rises from itself
appropriates bone/bent flesh
and stuns with its
juggernaut of joy

64

THE INNOCENTS

I

Against the grate
of G-major, your
notes take flight
like birdsong at the
birth of light
no day can measure

Melody held
between wing and the
wing's wedging
of air, you sail
the sky's endless
edge against
                    gravity

65

2

Such innocence
cannot be borrowed
and set to lyric ends,
cannot be lent
or feigned (alas)
to mend with music
those sorrows we
open to it in
perpetual expectation

It is the gift
of song itself,
of singing
in the singer

Nor does it bring us
the sweet unclutter
of Eden's engendering,
the child's unsubtle
seeing we all
pretend to love
or regret the passing of—

The innocence I hear is
dark with the knowledge
of what has been lost/
forgotten/surrendered
to sentiment or art,

but oh, your voice
carries its terrible news
high and sweet and tender
into the uncompromising sky
our secret hearts
reach out to . . . .

3

You were born
one of those few
lyric choristers who
bore witness to
earth's breech-birth, the
first leaching of light,
who saw and sang and
made remembrance
                         your vow:

    the lark, homeless
    in his meadow
    transfiguring pain
    into panegyric

    the robin, alone
    at dawn
    murmuring her pro-
    and epithalamion

HOME

I

This season *hillbilly* is
camp, quaint as
Granny's damson jam
it suits our city passion
for matters country and
local, exotic and
downhome-ish

Yesteryear you all
were bug-eyed idiots
slouched with shotgun
(or peasant-breasted)
grinning your peculiar
untouchable malice
outward at silly tourists
lost in the maze
of interbred back-
woodsy lanes

69

Only your music
tells the whole
story, it cannot lie
even when it wants to,
there's no disguise
for truth in the
corruptive twanging and
nasal sentimentalities
we have appropriated
with virtuous civility—

the voice within
the singing within
the singer reaches
                    thru
and makes us listen
as if song herself
were the eldest muse
on earth
            and new

And you, Loretta,
make memorable
again your own
ancestral earthsong:
the skirl of Celtic
rage in Boadicea's
cry, her valleys
ravaged by Tuscan
campmongers, the
glee-wail of
Irish fife in the
muffling green glens,
the harp in Arthur's halls
condensing heaven in the
wake of Saxon drums,
the tom-tom's muted
lament for the lost
forever Cherokee hills,
the fiddle's hopscotch
skipping-rope dance
on your father's hand-
made floorboards, a
mother's timeless lullabies
filling the only room
any of us can ever
    call home.

SAID AND DONE

I

What misanthropic muse
prompted you (child
bride and pregnant with
Melpomene's promise)
to put such Oregons
between you and the
father who loved you
more than his life
dragged daily thru the
bituminous blood-seam
beneath the earth's
green he watched you
bloom in . . . .

And when the coal's
bonds claimed him,
only then did your
music utter its
surrogate grief in
ballad, lament,
honky-tonk dirge—
the upward edge of
song itself gone
underground in quest of
the love we possess
only in absence.

2

I picture your father
like my own in an
old man's kitchen:
crippled smile, the
unquenchable eye
shrivelling, aimed
at itself,
       but *yours*
never left loving:

you, pain, even the
loathsome hutch of
flesh we suffer
our last days in,
the distance between you
becomes the measure
of your adoration

3

But *mine* left loving,
living and the un-
claimed spaces between
(father: the eye you cast
upon your son swallowed
its own spark,
welcomed in
the embezzling dark)

Is it rage, then,
self-mockery, some
quirk of love's
underground urgency
that propels these
word-meshed metaphors
across the bride-
shy blush of the
                    page?

After all is said,
a simple hello
how are you
I love you
would have done.

GRATITUDE

In this tri-lit
amber after-
evening room
your songs slip
their rhymes and carry
us to country
fairs in Brigden, to
midnight skates on
ponds crisper than the
moon's eyeball, to
muskrat hunts in the
libidinous dance of
April creeks (Dad's
grin rooted in mine),
to summering beaches
forsaken once by
Attawandarons the
girls with a season's
heat in their bones
didn't care   I
headed home to my
grandmother's kitchen
already fading
in the autumn
haze over Brigden
where prize bulls
preened and curried
acclamation.

Even now, this very
second (as your lyric
frames my mother's
smile retrieved from
years you wouldn't
acknowledge nor let
me thank you for)
you may be riding
some numberless highway
in the numb half of night
where no music relieves
the migrainous dream
of miles without meaning,
and the three-headed ulcer
turns over in your sleep.

76

ALPHABETS

I

Once more I watch
the film that tries to
free you from cliché,
pin down the essential
myth, make you more
and less than you were,
and somehow misses the
point

    you

were more than a
country balladeer
anthologizing your
father's lost eyes
no song could assuage
with its ersatz hope and
public good-cheer so
prized in the bistros
you praise and deny.

And less than a
daughter-of-the-dialect
savagely noble in her
hollows and coombes
untinctured by time
or the brutal sloughs
of suburb and alley:
    the Hollywood dream
    of our death's flesh
    resurrected in the
    random blue crocus,
    the green incarnation
    of the local.

2

You were and are
simply yourself,
surprised by the songs
that spring like iambic
from a bard's tongue,
stunned by their
wonder, by the flawed
marble of their
making in the
sweet/hurt/lost/loving
crucible no
words can touch
with their tremor.

Though I try—
because you too
are one of the poets
doomed by lot
to probe with a
ferret's stare
the foetal dens
where earth's urgings
fester, and blazon
the alphabets of poetry
　　　　　　and despair.